EPILEPSY

EPILEPSY

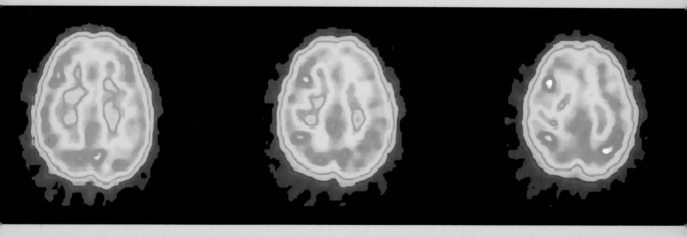

Ruth Bjorklund

Marshall Cavendish
Benchmark
New York

For Lily

Marshall Cavendish Benchmark
99 White Plains Road
Tarrytown, New York 10591-9001
www.marshallcavendish.us

Library of Congress Cataloging-in-Publication Data

Bjorklund, Ruth.
 Epilepsy / by Ruth Bjorklund.
   p. cm. -- (Health alert)
 Summary: "Explores the history, causes, symptoms, treatments, and future
of epilepsy and seizure disorders"--Provided by publisher.
 Includes index.
 ISBN-13: 978-0-7614-2206-8
 ISBN-10: 0-7614-2206-4
 1. Epilepsy--Juvenile literature. I. Title. II. Series: Health alert (New York, N.Y.)

 RC372.2.B56 2007
 616.8'53--dc22

                                    2006015816

Photo research by Candlepants, Inc.
Front cover: Scott Camazine / Photo Researchers, Inc.
The photographs in this book are used by permission and through the courtesy of:
PhotoTake.com: Dr. M.O. Habert, Pitie-Salpetriere, 3, 18; BSIP, 41. *Photo Researchers Inc.:* James Cavallini, 5, 12; Jim Dowdalls, 13; Christian Darkin, 16; Science Source, 21; AJ Photo, 25; Phanie, 26, 43; Scott Camazine, 27; Josh Sher, 35. *Corbis:* LWA-Stephen Welstead, 23; Bettmann, 32; Hulton-Deutsch Collection, 33; Richard Bloom, 35; Jose Luiz Pelaez, Inc., 34; Gianni Dagli Orti, 45. *Art Resource, New York:* SCALA, 29. *The Image Works:* Mary Evans Picture Library, 30; Topham, 31, 44; Esbin-Anderson, 38; David Grossman, 53. *The Epilepsy Foundation:* 51, 55.

Printed in China
6 5 4 3 2 1

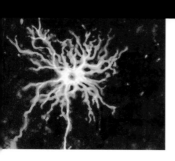

CONTENTS

1

WHAT IS IT LIKE TO HAVE EPILEPSY?

When Isabel was born, her brain was injured and before she was hours old, she began having **seizures,** which are sudden, abnormal electrical discharges in the brain. Isabel's seizures were what are known as **generalized seizures.** They affected her whole brain. When a seizure began, Isabel would turn her head to her left side, her eyes would blink rapidly, her right arm would jerk, and eventually her entire body would stiffen, and she would no longer be **conscious.** Isabel's doctors gave her special medication to stop the seizures, but they kept coming. So the doctors gave her more medication—enough to keep Isabel unconscious, until her brain calmed down.

Isabel stayed in the hospital for three months. When she came home, she was still taking seizure medication. The medication kept most of the seizures away, but they made Isabel very sleepy. By the time she was a year old, Isabel was strong and healthy. So her parents wanted to find a better medication to control Isabel's seizures—one that would not make her so tired.

One day, Isabel was visiting friends when she had an unexpected seizure. Isabel's doctor told her parents to give her a larger dose of the medication. But twenty minutes after they gave her more, Isabel went wild. Her face became red, and she ran around the room. She was out of control—laughing, crying, waving her arms, and not stopping. This had never happened in the past when Isabel was given this medication. So the doctor suggested a new medication. But it seemed that when she took it, Isabel had more seizures than ever before. With the doctor's help, Isabel's family tried to find the right dose, or amount, of medication to give. But it did not help, and Isabel's seizures changed. Isabel started having **absence seizures.** During one of these seizures, Isabel would just stare off into space and not have any idea what she was doing. For example, if she was playing in her sandbox and had an absence seizure, she would just continue to pour sand and stare off into space. Isabel's parents were unhappy with how the medication was working and decided to bring Isabel to a different doctor.

The new doctor agreed that Isabel's medication might not be helping, and might even be making her seizures worse. He started Isabel on a new medication to see if it would help her. Isabel had far fewer seizures with the new medication, but she seemed less alert. And when she did have a seizure, it took a whole day for her to recover from it. When the seizures ended, she was tired, her muscles ached, her stomach felt queasy, and she only wanted to sleep.

Isabel was a cheerful, otherwise healthy girl, but the medication interfered with her ability to pay attention in school. So Isabel and her family went to the doctor to see what could be done to help Isabel stay focused in class. He suggested not taking the medication. For the past few years, Isabel had three to six seizures a year. The doctor wanted to see if not taking the medication would increase the number of her seizures or not make a difference at all. Isabel and her family decided to try this out.

Isabel stopped taking the medication and over the next few years, she had less than six seizures each year. Her seizures always came when she was sick or tired—either just as she was going to sleep or right after she awoke. She learned to sense when the seizures were coming and would try to find her parents so that they could help her during the seizures.

Early one morning, Isabel had a seizure that would not stop. After ten minutes, her parents grew frightened and called 911. The paramedics gave Isabel a shot of a medication called diazepam, which put her to sleep and stopped the seizure. Isabel was also taken to the hospital where doctors and specialists could observe her recovery. At the end of the day, Isabel and her family were able to go home. But from then on, everyone was nervous about Isabel's seizures. What if another one started and did not stop? The family stopped taking vacations away from the city. They were too afraid to go camping, boating, or hiking in the woods, which had been some of their favorite activities. "What if Isabel had a seizure that we cannot stop while we are up in the mountains? What do we do then?" they worried. They considered putting Isabel back on medications, but she was doing so well in school without them. So Isabel and her family decided to keep doing what they were doing and hope for the best.

Over the next two years, Isabel only had seven seizures, but three of them would not stop. For those seizures paramedics had to be called to help her. Finally, Isabel's doctor suggested that her parents learn how to give Isabel the diazepam themselves. He instructed them how to inject the medicine and how to watch for **side effects.** Once they knew how to help Isabel during the unstoppable seizures, her family felt much better.

Isabel and her family took their vacations together and did all the things they wanted to do. Today Isabel is a happy and healthy young woman. She still has seizures, but she does not let her condition control her life.

2

WHAT IS EPILEPSY?

Epilepsy is the name given to a group of brain disorders. It is a very common illness and affects about 2.5 million American men, women, and children. Epilepsy affects nearly 50 million people worldwide. It can appear at any age, but most often children and older adults develop the disease.

There are many types of epilepsy, ranging from mild to serious. There are several causes for the condition, and it can affect anyone. Among the people who have epilepsy, symptoms can vary greatly. However, everyone who has the illness experiences seizures. Because of this, epilepsy is sometimes called a seizure disorder.

THE NERVOUS SYSTEM

The human nervous system is made up of different parts: nerves, the brain, and the spinal cord. This system is responsible for many bodily functions, including breathing, feeling, moving, thinking, and talking. The nervous system is one of the most complex parts of the human body. Much of it is still a mystery to doctors and scientists. Learning about the nervous system is important in order to understand epilepsy.

The brain and spinal cord are composed of microscopic units called nerve cells. There are two main types of nerve cells: **neurons** and **glial** cells. The role of neurons is to send and receive messages that control all of the body's senses, emotions, movements, and functions. Neurons are made of three

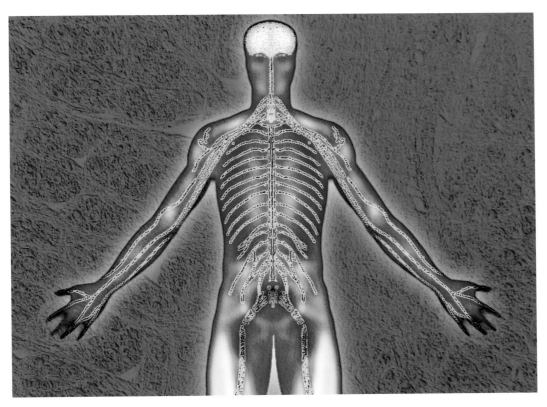

Computer artwork shows how parts of the nervous system reach throughout the body. The Central Nervous System (or CNS) is made up of the brain and the spinal cord.

main parts: the body, **dendrites,** and the **axon.** The body, or **soma,** guides the cell and contains the cell's information. Dendrites branch out from the soma and receive information from other neurons. The axon is a tail-like structure that sends out this information to other neurons. At the end of each axon is a bulge called the axon terminals. They send out the messages. The tips of the axon terminals do not touch other nerve cells. There is a gap between them called a **synapse** or a synaptic gap. Each axon has 1,000 to 10,000 synapses around it. This means that each neuron can send a message to that many other neurons.

The messages sent by neurons are carried through chemicals called **neurotransmitters.** Neurotransmitters travel down the axon, through the axon terminals, and cross the synapses to nearby neurons. Dendrites on the other neurons receive the message.

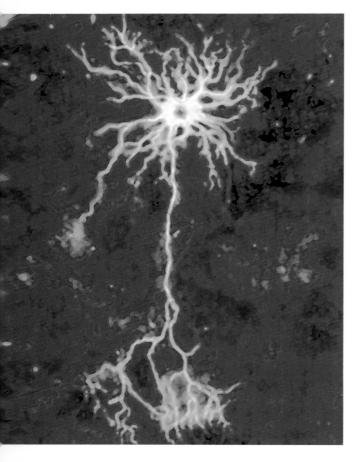

A human neuron. Millions of neurons in your body are responsible for helping to keep you alive and healthy.

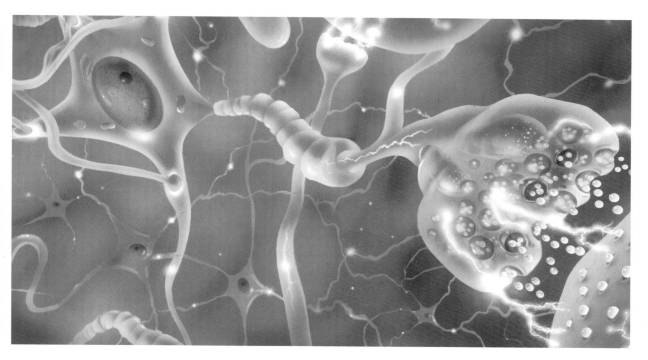

Neurotransmitters travel from the axon to the dendrites of nearby neurons. The little round spheres in this illustration are the neurotransmitters.

Sometimes the neurotransmitters will excite the nearby nerve cells, and sometimes they will inhibit them, or calm them down.

There are about 100 billion nerve cells in the brain. Ninety percent of them are glial cells. These cells do not send out neurotransmitters. Instead, they provide support for other nerves and the brain. They also provide nourishment and help to remove waste and dead cells.

Neurons, glial cells, and other nerve cells form bundles called nerves. Together, the nerves and the brain send and receive messages throughout the nervous system. The human nervous system has two sections: central and peripheral. The central nervous system is made up of the brain and the spinal cord. The spinal cord runs up the middle of a person's back—from around the hips to the brain. It is protected by the bones that make up the spine. Nerves in the body deliver messages to and from the brain through the nerves in the spinal cord.

The peripheral nervous system is made up of nerves that carry information to and from the rest of the body and the central nervous system. For example, if you touch a hot stove with your finger, peripheral nerves in your finger will send the sensation of heat to the nerves in the spinal cord. Those nerves will then transmit the sensory information to your brain. Your brain will process the information and send more information back to the spinal cord. That message will travel through the spinal cord to the peripheral nerves leading to your finger. You will experience pain in your finger and your body will react by pulling the finger away from the stove. In most healthy people, this message relay and the body's response will take only a fraction of a second.

THE BRAIN

The brain has three main parts: the hindbrain, midbrain, and forebrain. Each part controls certain body functions. The hindbrain includes the cerebellum, the **pons,** and the medulla oblongata. The medulla connects to the spinal cord and controls unconscious body functions such as breathing, swallowing, vomiting, and heart rate. The pons relays messages from other parts of the brain and is also active in controlling sleep. The cerebellum is important to muscle movement, balance, and coordination. The midbrain is an area of the brain that filters sensory information and connects the forebrain to the hindbrain. The pons, medulla, and the midbrain make up what is called the brain stem.

The forebrain, which includes the cerebrum, is the largest and most complex part of the brain. Inside the forebrain is a brain system called the limbic system. This part of the brain controls feelings and emotions, such as fear, anger, pleasure, hunger, and thirst.

The most advanced part of the cerebrum is called the cerebral cortex. The cortex is divided into two halves called the right hemisphere and left hemisphere. The right hemisphere controls the left side of the body, and the left hemisphere controls the right side of the body.

Each hemisphere has four parts, called lobes: the frontal, parietal, occipital, and temporal lobes. The frontal lobe controls behavior, thought, movement, creativity, problem solving, judgment, and sense of smell. The parietal lobe manages the sense of touch, some speech and language skills, and also interprets other sensations. The occipital lobe is responsible for reading and vision. The temporal lobe oversees hearing, sense of fear, music awareness, and some parts of emotions, speech, language, and memory.

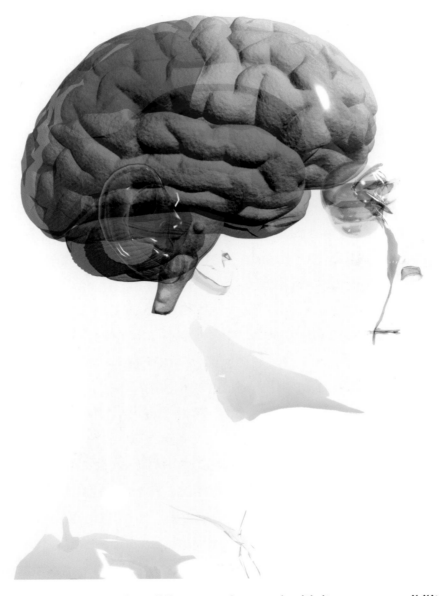

The human brain is divided into different sections, each with its own responsibilities. The yellow portion is the frontal lobe, the green is the temporal lobe, the pink is the parietal lobe, and the occipital lobe is shown in red. The brain stem is colored in orange and the cerebellum is colored dark blue.

Seizures and the Brain

When the brain is functioning normally, it produces electrical signals and chemical reactions that travel along nerves throughout the body. The brain controls the body's movements, thoughts, and emotions. It also receives and interprets information, stores thoughts and ideas as memory, and allows us to touch, see, hear, taste, and smell.

Normally, neurons send electrical signals at a rate that is under 100 times per second. During an epileptic seizure, neurons send electrical signals extremely fast—sometimes as many as 500 times per second. This can happen in one small part of the brain or it can occur throughout the entire brain. When the signals come too fast, they send messages that force the body to react in an uncontrollable way. During some seizures, people may simply stare or blink for a few seconds. Other people undergoing a seizure may have very intense movements, fall to the ground, or become unconscious for several minutes. Some people have only one type of seizure, while others can experience different types.

TYPES OF SEIZURES

Seizures have a variety of causes, such as a brain injury, a chemical imbalance in the body, a brain tumor (an abnormal growth), a brain infection, or drug and alcohol abuse. Some causes of seizures are completely unknown. Most seizures occur

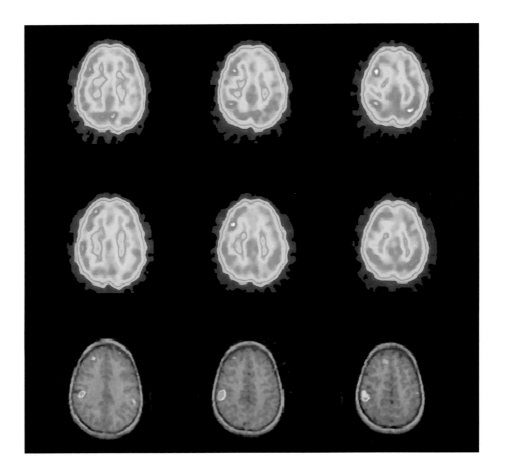

These scans are from the brain of a two-year-old child with partial epilepsy. The top rows show the brain during a seizure. The bottom row shows in which part of the brain the seizures are occurring.

in the cerebrum. Exactly where a seizure begins is called a focus. The focus determines how a person behaves during the start of a seizure. There are two main types of seizures. **Partial seizures** start in a particular part of the brain, but may spread to other parts. Generalized seizures affect the whole brain all at once.

Partial Seizures

Partial seizures are the most common. In a partial seizure, the abnormal electrical activity stays within one hemisphere of the brain. People with epilepsy usually sense when one of these seizures is about to begin. This feeling is called an **aura.**

Partial seizures can be simple or complex. In a simple partial seizure, the person stays awake, although he or she may be unable to speak or control his or her body. Depending on where the focus is, a person may shake a finger or leg, stare straight ahead, have facial twitches, sense a sinking feeling in the stomach, or hear, feel, taste, or see something that is not really there. Some people may laugh, cry, feel cold, or begin sweating. Any part of the body or any sense or emotion can be affected.

In a complex partial seizure, the electrical activity involves a larger portion of the brain. People with complex partial seizures may seem like they are awake, but they are not fully aware of what is going on around them. Although their eyes are open, they are in a trancelike state and will not remember what happened during the seizure. Complex partial seizures usually begin in the temporal lobe of the brain. Most people who have them begin by staring. Then, they may smack their lips or make chewing movements, run or walk around aimlessly, cry, babble, or wave their arms. They appear confused or frightened. In both types of partial seizures, the seizure may advance to include more of the brain, like a generalized seizure.

Generalized Seizures

Generalized seizures affect both hemispheres of the brain when they start. There are four main types of generalized seizures: absence, **atonic, myoclonic,** and **tonic-clonic.** Absence seizures were also once known as *"petit mal"* seizures, which is French for "small sickness." Children are more likely to have this type of seizure than adults, and some children may have as many as one hundred of these seizures a day. During an absence seizure, people may stare, flutter their eyelids, or their muscles may twitch. The seizure is very brief and people do not feel anything before or after.

An atonic seizure is sometimes called a "drop attack" because the seizure is quick and very sudden and people often fall as their muscles give way. People who have myoclonic seizures experience rapid muscle jerks on both sides of their body.

The most common generalized seizure is the tonic-clonic seizure, once called a *"grand mal"* seizure, which is French for "big sickness." When a tonic-clonic seizure begins, people will stiffen their arms and legs, and then jerk them about wildly. People having a tonic-clonic seizure lose consciousness and their breathing becomes irregular. Some turn slightly blue from lack of oxygen. They may cry out, move their mouths in a chewing pattern, or sometimes bite their tongue. After this type of seizure ends, people usually have a headache and are tired, sore, and confused. Most people want to sleep afterward, and it often takes several hours to recover.

TYPES OF EPILEPSY

Types of epilepsy are different from types of seizures. There are many types of epilepsy, such as juvenile myoclonic, childhood absence, benign rolandic, reflex, and Lennox-Gastaut. Juvenile myoclonic epilepsy begins between ages eight and fourteen. They have many types of seizures, usually in the morning.

Children who develop childhood absence epilepsy begin having seizures between the ages of four and eight. They will have brief staring spells, sometimes as many as fifty times a day. This type of epilepsy runs in families and many people outgrow the disorder.

In benign rolandic epilepsy, children can have tonic-clonic seizures in their sleep. When they are awake they may have

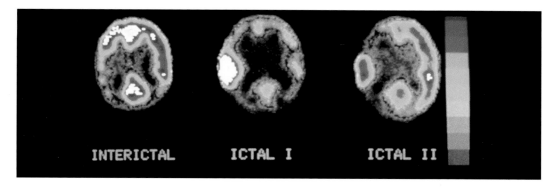

INTERICTAL   ICTAL I   ICTAL II

This scan shows the brain during an epileptic seizure. The brighter colors represent higher brain activity because the neurons are firing rapidly.

partial seizures, usually affecting the face. It gets its name from an area called the rolandic strip located in the temporal and parietal lobes of the brain. This strip controls the face. Benign rolandic epilepsy is often outgrown by the age of fifteen.

Reflex epilepsy is caused by triggers in the environment, such as flickering lights, television or video game screens, sounds, music, a certain person's voice, colors, a hot bath, or a back rub. The most common reflex epilepsy is from flashing lights and television screens. People with this type of epilepsy respond by having tonic-clonic, absence, or myoclonic seizures.

There are other epilepsy forms that can be very serious. Many of these are a result of a brain injury or brain disorder. Lennox-Gastaut is one such type of epilepsy and people who have this type have many different types of seizures. They may have tonic-clonic seizures that do not stop on their own, and require emergency medical treatment.

DIAGNOSING EPILEPSY

Some people are born with epilepsy, while others develop the disease later in life. But once a person has had a seizure, he or she should see a doctor and have a complete medical examination. The doctor will do an examination and run tests. Based on those results a doctor may **diagnose** a person with epilepsy.

The first part of the examination is often performed by a primary care or general physician. This is a doctor who will check the patient's overall health and order laboratory tests for the patient's blood, liver, kidneys, heart, and other organs. When the doctor suspects epilepsy, he or she will refer the patient to a neurologist. This is a doctor who is specially trained in **neurology,** which is the branch of medicine that deals with the nervous system and its disorders.

During a neurological examination, the neurologist will test the patient's reflexes, muscle movement, senses, thinking, and memory. The doctor will check eye movements and facial expressions. If the patient is able, the doctor may ask the patient to run, walk, or stand on one foot. The neurologist may also ask the patient

Part of a neurological exam includes testing reflexes. A neurologist might use a tool called a reflex hammer to check the way your nerves and muscles respond to certain stimulation.

to answer math or spelling questions. Next, the neurologist will take down the patient's medical history. This often includes questions about health problems or seizure disorders a patient's

Medical Questions

....

These are some of the questions a neurologist might ask a patient when trying to diagnose epilepsy:

- How often do you have seizures and how long do they last?
- What happens during your seizures?
- What were you doing right before the seizure?
- Do you feel any warning signs before seizures begin?
- How do you feel afterward—tired or confused? Can you speak after a seizure? Do you have a headache, stomachache, or muscle aches?
- How long is it before you feel and act normally again?

The answers to these questions help the neurologist determine what types of seizures the patient experiences, what type of epilepsy the patient has, and how they can treat it.

family members might have had. The neurologist will also ask about events before and after the patient's seizures. This part of the exam may take some time, as families try to piece together what they remember about the stressful events surrounding the patient's seizures. Often, the medical history part takes place over many visits.

To better understand the patient's needs, the neurologist will also order tests, usually beginning with an EEG. EEG stands for **electroencephalograph,** and it is a type of test that shows patterns of electrochemical activity in the brain. An EEG can also help a doctor identify the parts of the brain where electrical activity is abnormal. An EEG is painless and the person undergoing the test is usually very relaxed or sleepy. Medical technicians stick electrodes to different parts of the person's head. These electrodes are special sensors that read electrical activity in the brain.

A young girls undergoes an EEG to monitor the electrical activity in her brain. The monitor shows her brain waves during an epileptic seizure.

As the patient is asked to do various things, such as eye blinking or deep breathing, the electrodes will sense the brain's electrical activity and send the information to the rest of the EEG machine. The brain's activity is recorded as squiggly lines or waves. EEG technicians and neurologists can "read" these waves and analyze the patient's brain activity. While the EEG does not necessarily detect epilepsy, it can help the doctor identify what form of epilepsy the patient has.

Other commonly used tests are CAT scans—sometimes called CT scans—or MRI scans. These scans take special pictures of parts of the body—in this case, the brain. In a CT scan, the patient lays his or her head in a special cradle, and as the cradle slowly re-positions the head, the scanner takes pictures. In an MRI, the patient lays on a special bed that is placed inside a machine. The machine uses magnets and other

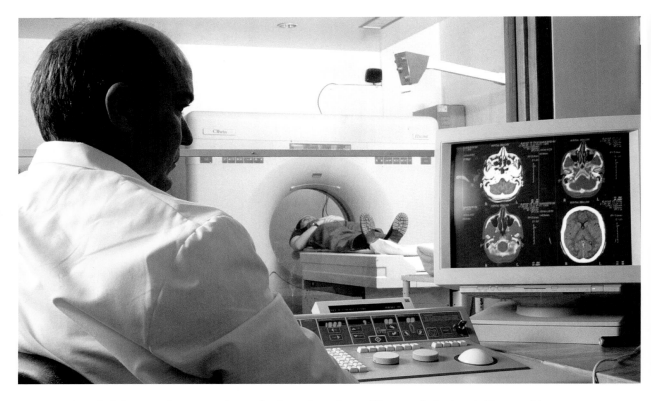

A technician monitors a patient who is undergoing a CT scan of the head. The machine scans the person's head and creates an image of the brain for technicians and doctors to examine.

technology to create an image of the brain. CT scans and MRIs may reveal brain injuries or other physical problems with the brain. These problems may be causing the seizures.

Sometimes neurologists may have their patients undergo a PET scan. A PET scan gives doctors information about chemical changes and blood flow in the brain during seizures. However, the machines for PET scans are often very expensive and not all medical centers have them.

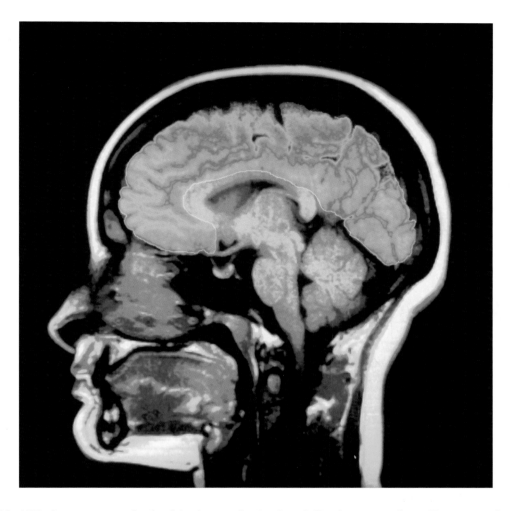

This MRI shows a scan of a healthy human brain. Specialized scans such as CT scans and MRIs help doctors identify damage to the brain or abnormal brain activity.

In addition to these tests, some doctors will observe a patient during a seizure. Once the doctor can clearly diagnose epilepsy and the type of seizures the patient is having, treatment can begin.

3

THE HISTORY OF EPILEPSY

More than 3,000 years ago in Mesopotamia—which included parts of present-day southwestern Asia—people believed that epilepsy was caused by the god of the moon. To others in ancient China, Egypt, India, and Greece, seizures were caused by devils, demons, and gods. Doctors of ancient times described the very same types of seizures as present-day doctors describe. But the ancients felt treatment should be spiritual.

Around 400 BCE, the Greek physician, Hippocrates, discussed epilepsy in a work called *The Sacred Disease*. In it, he rejected the notion that supernatural beings caused seizures and wrote that the disease, " . . . appears to me to be in no way more divine nor more sacred than other diseases . . . The brain is the cause of this affliction..." Hippocrates had the right idea about epilepsy being a disease of the brain, but those ideas were cast aside.

In the Middle Ages, around 500 to 1500 CE, people believed that people with epilepsy were bewitched. Instead of doctors, priests were called upon to treat patients. In the fourteenth and fifteenth centuries, the common treatment was a prayer called the Falling Sickness Blessing. Witch-hunters believed that a person who had seizures was most likely a witch. In 1692—the time of the Salem witch trials in the United States—people believed that seizures were a sign of witchcraft.

Everywhere around the world, societies were frightened of people who had seizures, and as a result, many people with epilepsy were mistreated. Although society turned against most people with epilepsy, some people with the disease were

This artwork is one of the most famous paintings showing a person with epilepsy (the boy at the bottom right corner). One reason the artist Raphael painted this religious picture was to show how many believed Jesus could heal people with epilepsy.

Until doctors understood what was happening to a person with epilepsy, most people did not know how to help or treat someone who was having a seizure.

honored because their seizures were thought to be messages from divine beings, such as saints or gods.

It was not until the late eighteenth century that doctors began to believe Hippocrates' idea that epilepsy was a disease of the brain. Still, most people were afraid they could catch the disease. So people with epilepsy usually spent their lives locked away in institutions. In the 1850s, many European countries established hospitals and asylums for people with epilepsy.

Around the 1850s, British doctor Sir Charles Locock began

British physician Sir Charles Locock helped to develop one of the first medications used to treat seizures.

using bromide—a chemical mixture—as a drug to treat seizures. It quieted the brain and was the first medication to truly help people with the disease. Later, in 1873, a doctor named John Hughlings Jackson noted that seizures were caused by sudden electrochemical impulses in the brain. One form of seizure that begins at a focal point and moves throughout the brain is named after Jackson. This type of seizure is called a "Jacksonian March."

By the end of the nineteenth century, doctors were on the right track to helping people with the disease and understanding that epilepsy was a neurologic disorder. In the 1920s, a psychiatrist named Hans Berger developed the electroencephalograph. As a result, doctors were better able to monitor brain activity.

MODERN ADVANCES
Since the early twentieth century, more successful drugs have been created to help people with epilepsy. These medications

Throughout history, many people have advertised false cures for diseases such as epilepsy. This advertisement shows an electric belt that was supposed to end epileptic seizures. It did not work.

can help to control their seizures so that they can live as normally as possible. Phenobarbital was developed in 1912, and it helped calm the brain. However, too much makes patients sleepy or anxious. Also, people can become addicted to phenobarbital. It is still a medication taken today, but there are more than twenty other, newer anti-epileptic drugs, which are sometimes called AEDs. AEDs usually work best by targeting just one or two types of seizures. Some people who have several different types of seizures usually take more than one medication. Dosages have to be carefully managed so that the drugs do not interfere with other drugs or cause too many unpleasant side effects. "The brain is still a mystery," says Dr. William Graf, a neurologist in Kansas City. "Sometimes we

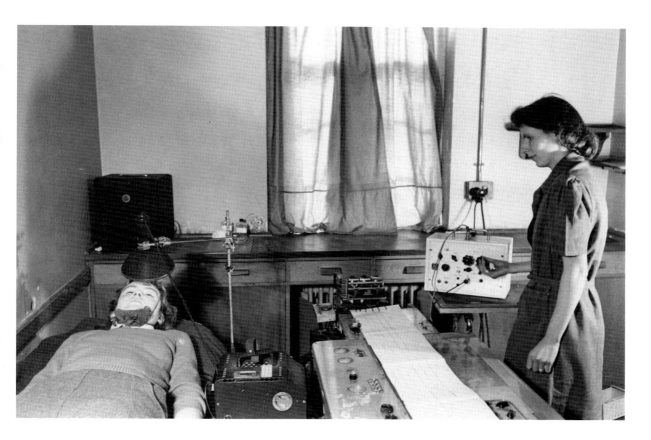

A scientist uses an early version of an EEG machine to measure the brain waves of a man with epilepsy. The brain waves were recorded as squiggly lines on long sheets of paper.

don't know why certain drugs work. But when they do, the patient's quality of life improves. And that's what we want to see."

Technological advances also led to the creation of CT scans, MRIs, and PET scans. With these tools, doctors could do more to help their patients. Modern-day advancements in the research and treatment of epilepsy have given today's patients greater freedom to live normal lives.

BECOMING SEIZURE-FREE

In 2000, the National Institutes of Neurological Disorders and Stroke held an international meeting about epilepsy. Doctors, researchers, scientists, and patients from around the world gathered to discuss new ways of treating the disease. They decided to focus on developing new medications, and improving treatment in areas such as surgery, cell transplants, vaccinations, and electronic implants. They also pledged to seek a cure for epilepsy, rather than just improving treatment for patients. Together, these doctors, researchers, technicians, and patients have a new goal. They are working toward curing a serious disease that has troubled people for thousands of years.

By working together and sharing information, new discoveries, and new technologies, someday people with epilepsy around the world will be able to receive helpful treatments.

A Champion for Americans with Disabilities

In the 1960s, a California teenager named Tony Coelho was in a car accident and struck his head on the ground. Soon after, he started having seizures and was eventually diagnosed with epilepsy. Because of his epilepsy, the state took away his driver's license and he lost his health insurance. Coelho became very angry, stopped working hard, and stopped taking care of himself.

But meeting with the famous comedian Bob Hope helped turn Coelho around. Hope hired him to do odd jobs and later introduced him to a California congressman named Bernie Sisk. Sisk hired Coelho and gave him support and guidance. Coelho became Sisk's assistant and worked in the congressman's office in Washington, D.C.

In 1978, Tony Coelho was elected to the U.S. House of Representatives. He quickly became a leading member of his political party. But his good fortune did not cause Tony Coelho to forget his troubled youth.

In one speech Coelho said, "Time hasn't healed my scars or erased the painful memories. But, over the years, I have learned to carry them as a mark of pride in who I am and what I can accomplish, as a person with a disability."

In Congress, he worked to help other disabled Americans find jobs and lead normal lives. Tony Coelho was the main author of the laws that became known as the Americans with Disabilities Act (ADA). Today, this act provides protection for Americans with disabilities. By law, they cannot be unfairly treated because of their disabilities.

4

LIVING WITH EPILEPSY

In the United States and in many other countries, most people with epilepsy are able to live healthy and active lives. With the help of expert medical care and the right medications, 80 percent of epilepsy patients are free to experience nearly all that life has to offer.

TREATING EPILEPSY WITH MEDICATION

Many people suffering from seizures are given anti-epileptic drugs. Taking daily medication is the most common treatment for epilepsy. There are many anti-epileptic drugs, and they each work in different ways to stop, prevent, or lessen seizures. Ideally, patients need to take only one medication. However, in more serious cases where many types of seizures are present, a patient may have to take a combination of drugs. Often, the patient, the patient's family, and the neurologist will have to work together to make sure that the dosage—or amount of medication—is right and that the medication provides the most help with the fewest side effects.

Choosing the right medication can take some time. When a patient begins a new anti-epileptic medication, doctors guide their patients through a process called a drug trial. In a drug trial, patients follow a strict schedule. They begin by taking a small amount of the medication. Over the course of days and weeks, they gradually increase the dosage to a full therapeutic dose. A therapeutic dose is the lowest dose of medication that achieves the best possible results. Unless serious side effects occur right away, doctors usually advise their patients to try the drug for at least six weeks. Possible side

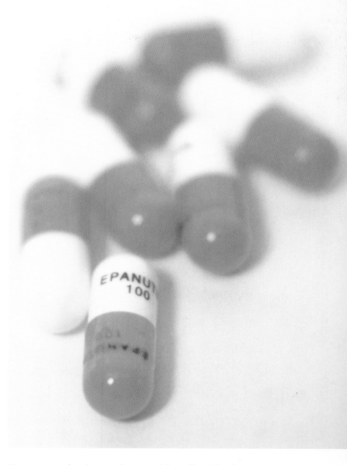

Many people depend on anti-epileptic drugs to help control their seizures.

effects may include weight gain or loss, slurred speech, trouble concentrating, dizziness, jerking movements, unsteadiness, blurred vision, depression, insomnia (the inability to sleep), headaches, nausea, rashes, or damage to the blood, liver, or kidneys.

Careful doctor supervision is needed whenever anybody—at any age—is trying medication or any other form of medical treatment.

After the drug trial period, the doctor and patient will decide together whether or not to continue taking the drug. If the drug does not help control seizures well enough, or if the side effects are too uncomfortable, the patient will slowly stop taking the drug and try a new one. Nearly all anti-epileptic medications must be started and removed slowly, or they can disturb the brain and cause additional seizures.

Sometimes, people do not like the side effects and will skip a dosage of medication. If this happens, a harmful condition called *status epilepticus* can occur. This is when a seizure starts and does not stop. (*Status epilepticus* can also occur during any seizure.) When a seizure does not stop after ten minutes or more, emergency measures must be used and an ambulance should be called. When the ambulance arrives, the paramedics will usually give the patient a strong medication that will put them to sleep and stop the seizures. They will also give the patient oxygen and transport the patient to the nearest hospital for an exam. But if *status epilepticus* happens frequently, then involving emergency medical care might be unnecessary. Doctors will sometimes instruct the patient's family how to give the medication themselves. This can help the patient maintain a normal lifestyle with fewer trips to the hospital. Says one mother from Idaho, "We could finally plan to take our dream trip sailing as a family, knowing we had the means to stop our daughter's seizures if she had any. Now we will all be able to relax and enjoy ourselves!"

"Quality of life is the issue," remarks neurologist William Graf. "Patients have to decide for themselves how many seizures they are willing to have each year before they choose to take a daily medication. How many days of school are you willing to miss? What side effects are acceptable? What ones are not? If the medication makes you anxious, tired, or unable to concentrate, is it worth it to be seizure-free? These are all tough choices." As Dr. Graf points out, some people with mild forms of epilepsy may prefer not to take medication as long as they do not have seizures on most days. For others, anti-epileptic drugs are the key to a normal life.

OTHER TREATMENTS

Twelve-year-old Annie has had seizures her entire life. She has tried every anti-epileptic available. She and her parents have dutifully followed many drug trials. They have also tried combinations of medications. Sometimes the seizures seem under control, but then she has what her doctor calls a breakthrough seizure. This is a seizure that breaks through the medication, allowing other seizures to follow.

At one point, her family agreed that one seizure a month was acceptable. Then, the seizures came more often. Without much warning, Annie would fall to the floor, in a generalized, tonic-clonic seizure. "It's been so hard," said Annie's teacher. "She had been doing so well, and suddenly she started having drop seizures. She's fallen and broken so many teeth, and now, she has to wear a helmet all the time." So Annie's parents and doctors decided to try a different approach.

Vagus nerve stimulation, or VNS, is one of only a few non-drug treatments for epilepsy. VNS requires a small surgical operation. The vagus nerve is a very long nerve that winds through a person's upper body and sends signals to the brain. Research has shown that some people with epilepsy benefit when the vagus nerve is stimulated.

To stimulate the nerve, surgeons implant a tiny generator under the skin. During the operation, doctors connect small wires from the generator and attach them to the vagus nerve. These wires will remain under the skin. After the surgery, a doctor will use a computer and program the generator to stimulate the vagus nerve for about thirty seconds every five

The different pieces of the VNS are shown in this package. This small generator helps many people control their epileptic seizures.

minutes. When the nerve is stimulated, a patient will usually feel a slight tingling and his or her voice will become hoarse. Some patients find that when the generator regularly stimulates the nerve, they have fewer seizures.

Patients who are undergoing VNS also keep a strong magnet with them all the time, usually on a bracelet. The magnet does two things. First, a person can hold the magnet over the area where the generator lays beneath the skin. This action stops the stimulation. A person might want to stop the stimulation to avoid having his or her voice become hoarse—for example, if he or she wanted to sing or do public speaking.

The second thing the magnet can do is help prevent or reduce the seriousness of a seizure. If a person feels a seizure coming on, he or she can pass the magnet over the generator. Doing so causes the generator to immediately send a signal to the nerve. This can also be done once the seizure has started. The sudden stimulation of the nerve will usually halt the seizure's progress. Patients usually show their family, friends, teachers, and others around them how to use the magnet to control a seizure, in case their seizure comes without warning and they need help.

Another non-drug method of controlling seizures is brain surgery. While this may sound scary, many people say this therapy has given them a fresh start. But very few patients can consider brain surgery as an option. Only those patients whose seizures begin in a specific part of the brain can benefit from the procedure. There are several different types of surgery performed to help patients with epilepsy. In some procedures, parts of the temporal lobe are removed. Other procedures involve cutting tiny slices in the brain to stop the spread of abnormal electrical signals, or cutting the connections between the two

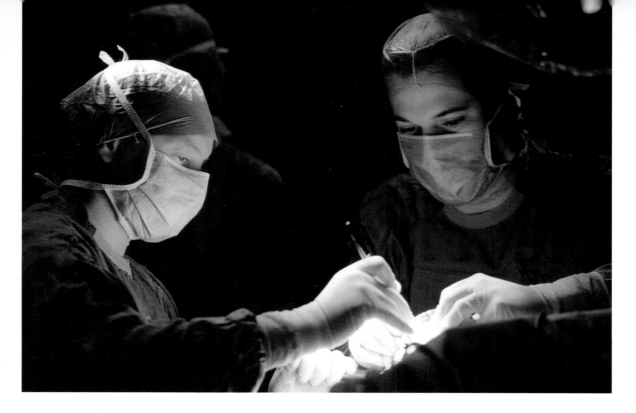

Sometimes patients and doctors decide that the only way to help a person with epilepsy is to perform some form of brain surgery. As with most surgeries, the risks are high, but many people feel that it is worth the relief from painful or disruptive seizures.

hemispheres of the brain. In another operation, when a patient has a tumor or other abnormal growth that causes seizures, surgeons remove the damaged brain tissue.

Most patients who have brain surgery continue to take medication, at least for awhile. Two-thirds of patients who have had surgery find their seizures controlled or even stopped. Many of them are able to stop taking daily medication. One patient who tried numerous drugs to control her uncontrollable seizures had successful surgery and wrote, "I wish surgery was the first resort and not the last!"

Seizure Dogs

A seizure dog is a service dog trained to help an owner who has seizures. There are two types of seizure dogs: seizure-assist dogs and seizure-alert dogs. Both types of seizure dogs require very careful training to do their job. A seizure-assist dog is trained to react when its owner has a seizure. Some dogs stay close to their owners to give them comfort and to provide a soft body to lean or fall against. Other dogs are trained to help their owners. They are taught to fetch medication, to get a caregiver or family member, or to push a special button that will dial 911.

A seizure alert dog is a rare animal. No one knows for sure why certain dogs seem to know when a person is about to have a seizure. But some dogs have the ability to sense that a person is going to have a seizure anytime between a few seconds to an hour before the seizure happens. Once they sense a seizure is

Chad, this five-year-old golden retriever, was honored as a Children's Companion of the Year for being able to predict his eleven-year-old owner's seizures. Seizure-alert and seizure-assist dogs are a great help to many people with epilepsy.

coming, these dogs alert their owner by barking, circling around, licking, or pawing. Some trainers believe that these dogs may sense slight changes in a person, such as a different body movement or scent. Breeds most commonly used as seizure dogs are Golden Retrievers and Labradors, yet other breeds and mixed breeds have also served their owners as life-saving seizure dogs and beloved companions.

Alternative Therapies

Alternative therapies are therapies that are not widely taught in medical schools and are not generally found in hospitals. Some alternative therapies work for many, but have not been rigorously tested or approved by government agencies that monitor healthcare. But some medical professionals today are more approving of alternative therapies, such as herbal medication and **acupuncture.** In fact, many people now call alternative therapies, "complementary therapies," which means that these therapies can sometimes work together with traditional medicine. Some people believe acupuncture can help calm

For over a thousand years, doctors have believed that specific herbs and plants can treat certain illnesses. This manuscript from the fourteenth century shows an herb that physicians at the time thought would cure epilepsy.

seizures in people with epilepsy, while others believe certain herbs can help. However, it is important for a person with epilepsy to tell his or her doctor about any alternative therapies he or she might be undergoing.

One popular alternative therapy for children with epilepsy is a diet called the ketogenic diet. This diet has been successful since the 1920s in treating some children with uncontrollable seizures. The diet "tricks" the body into feeling starved, and that causes the body to produce a chemical in the blood called a ketone. Ketones seem to control seizures. The diet is very strict, however. Children eat foods extremely high in fat, such as cheese, cream, bacon, nuts, and butter. They must take vitamins and avoid sweets, breads, and grains. This diet is unhealthy for most people, so children with epilepsy and their parents must have a doctor specially plan the diet for the child's age and weight. Every child on the ketogenic diet should always be under the careful watch of a medical doctor. Once a child is seizure-free for two to five years, the child can usually end the diet.

COPING WITH EPILEPSY

People with epilepsy and their families must learn to manage their illness, medication, and activities. Most people with epilepsy control their seizures with medication. But it is the responsibility of the patient, parents, and caregivers to be sure to follow medication guidelines. People with epilepsy and their families must be patient during drug trials, to give the medication a chance to take effect. On the other hand, when they are not satisfied with their medications, they need to give clear and honest feedback to their health-care providers.

Epilepsy support groups urge patients and their families to educate themselves as much as possible about their disease. Epilepsy patients should also wear a medical alert ID bracelet or anklet that clearly states that they have epilepsy. People with epilepsy should be open and honest about their disease with people they see everyday—friends, relatives, teachers, coaches, babysitters, and classmates. They should teach basic first aid and explain what a seizure is and what people should do and not do to help. Misunderstanding epilepsy leads to a lot of confusion and unhappiness. Although seizures may appear painful, frightening, or dangerous, they are generally none of those things. They are a symptom of a disease, just as a sneeze is a symptom of a cold.

Seizures come in many shapes and sizes. Sometimes a person having a seizure appears hysterical, clumsy, or very sick. Others may seem like they are misbehaving, daydreaming, or abusing drugs or alcohol. Of course, this is not the case. But classmates and others can be disturbed by what they see. When armed with information about seizures, teachers, school nurses, coaches, and others can keep everyone calm and remind classmates or teammates that the person having a seizure is only unable to control his or her body for a short time.

Seizures can look painful, and onlookers may want to offer help. If a child is having a seizure in school, for example, and only other children are around, someone should get an adult immediately. For the most part, letting the seizure run its course is all a person can do, though there are some things that ease the situation. When people have generalized seizures, the best way to help them is to speak calmly and gently guide them away from hazards, such as stairs or sharp corners. Sometimes, they may push or shove. They do not know they are doing this, so no one should take offense.

During generalized, clonic-tonic seizures do not try to restrain the person in any way, and do not put anything into the person's mouth. It was once believed that persons having such a seizure were in danger of swallowing their tongue, but this is not true. Adults who know how to assist people with tonic-clonic seizures can help them lie on their side and loosen any tight clothing. Any sharp objects close to the person should be removed. When the seizure is over, the person should be made comfortable since they will most likely need to rest.

An ambulance should be called if one is unsure that the person has epilepsy, if the seizure is longer than five minutes, if seizures stop and then begin again, or if the person appears injured or is not conscious afterward.

LIVING LIFE

Most people with epilepsy can do nearly anything that they want to do, but some things require extra care and attention.

Keeping a Seizure Diary

....

Keeping a seizure diary helps the patient and the doctor track the helpfulness of medications. It also may show a pattern to the seizures that could be useful in treating the disease. Families or witnesses should help with the diary, since patients may have trouble fully remembering what happens before, during, or after a seizure. Useful information to note includes:

- Date and time of the seizure
- Location
- Who else was there?
- Did you sense the seizure was coming? Did you have an aura?
- How did you feel just before the seizure—tired, sick, hot, sweaty, nervous, nauseous, dizzy, panicky, unable to breathe easily?
- Did you take alcohol, drugs, or prescription medication just before the seizure?
- What happened before, during, and after the seizure?
- How long did each stage last?
- Which parts of the body were affected and how?
- Did you lose consciousness?
- Can you remember the seizure?
- How long did it take you to be yourself again—right away, five minutes, an hour, the next day?
- Did you need to sleep afterward?
- When was your last dose of medication?
- What time was your next dose supposed to be?
- Had you forgotten to take a dose recently?

When playing sports, for example, soccer, tennis, baseball, softball, or basketball should be fine, as long as teammates and coaches know what to do if a seizure happens. Physical contact sports such as football, hockey, boxing, or some martial arts are usually too rough, especially for someone who has had a head injury.

A person who has epilepsy may be likely to experience seizures when they are tired or sick, so it is a good idea to avoid risky activity during those times. Some activities such as bike riding, skateboarding, skiing, snowboarding, and other sports should never be done alone. Since it is possible to become unconscious suddenly, it is necessary for a person with epilepsy to always wear a protective helmet while playing any sport. Rock climbing and hiking are also sports people with epilepsy should approach with caution, and never do alone.

Water sports have a special set of problems. Swimmers with epilepsy should always swim with a friend or adult. In the event of a seizure, the friend must hold the person's head above water until the seizure is over. Before swimming, swimmers should tell the lifeguards about their seizure disorder, and be sure the lifeguards know the right first aid. A person with epilepsy should never try sports such as scuba diving, parachuting, or auto racing. A seizure while participating in these sports could have serious consequences.

As children with epilepsy grow into adulthood, many may

The children in the picture visited Washington, D.C. in 2005 to participate in the Epilepsy Foundation's Kids Speak Up! Campaign. This program allows young "ambassadors" with epilepsy to encourage public awareness of problems associated with seizure disorders.

leave their seizures behind. But for some, seizures are part of their adult life. As adults, people with epilepsy have a new set of concerns. Adults with epilepsy should practice safety measures in their homes, such as padding sharp corners, buying furniture with rounded corners, cooking with a microwave when alone (instead of using a stove or oven), and not walking while carrying hot liquids, hot pans, or a hot iron. Driving a car can also be a challenge because a seizure can cause an accident. After having a seizure while driving, many individuals are not allowed to drive until they are seizure-free for at least a year. Unfortunately, this is often disappointing to the person with epilepsy and makes it more difficult for the person to attend school or go to work.

Laws in states around the country prevent most institutions and business from discriminating against a person with a disability. That means that a person with a disability, such as epilepsy, is protected under the law from being rejected from a school or turned away from a job based solely on the person's medical condition. But there are some jobs that a person with epilepsy cannot do, such as driving a bus or ambulance, being a police officer or a firefighter, and some construction or manufacturing jobs involving heavy machinery. Most people with epilepsy are not accepted into military service.

Women with epilepsy who want to have children may have to adjust their anti-epileptic medications. Under a doctor's care, however, women with epilepsy can have normal, healthy children, though they should take care to avoid becoming too tired, since that may trigger seizures.

The quality of life for people with epilepsy has greatly improved over the last century. Yet people with the disease, their families, researchers, and health-care workers look forward to a day when seizure medications and other treatments lead to a seizure-free life, or even a cure. More than fifty million people around the world have epilepsy. People with epilepsy

A technician observes the brain waves of a person with epilepsy. New technology and new discoveries have helped—and will continue to help—people with epilepsy live more comfortable and happy lives.

living in the United States and some other developed countries are luckier than most.

But most of the world's people with epilepsy live in developing countries without modern health-care systems. (A developing or undeveloped country is a place where there is much poverty and a lack of modern technological advances.) Unfortunately, the people with epilepsy in developing or undeveloped countries do not get proper diagnosis or treatment for their disease.

However, there are many organizations that are trying to

Famous People with Epilepsy

Many famous people have lived—or are believed to have lived—with epilepsy. It is one of the oldest recorded human health conditions. For the most part, the disease did not stop these people from accomplishing great things.

Alexander the Great, King of Macedonia

Julius Caesar, Emperor of Rome

Agatha Christie, Author

Charles Dickens, Author

Danny Glover, Actor

George Freidrich Handel, Composer

Florence Griffith Joyner, Athlete

Harriet Tubman, Underground Railroad Leader

Buddy Bell, Baseball player and coach

Neil Abercrombie, United States Congressman

Alfred, Lord Tennyson, Poet

change that. Organizations such as the International Bureau for Epilepsy and the International League Against Epilepsy are helping researchers share information about new medication. Epilepsy activists are spreading information about the disease and bringing medication to people without regular access to health care.

Many experts say that the greatest need is for education and compassionate understanding about the disease. Former U.S. congressman Tony Coelho adds that the greatest efforts should be spent on teaching young people about the disease, saying, "Our money should be spent working on kids. Kids with epilepsy and with kids in general about the *perception* of epilepsy. . . Kids are our future. Kids are our greatest resource . . . Young people with epilepsy need to know that they can succeed at whatever they want to do if they have a real desire."

Having a seizure disorder will not stop many young people from living their lives and pursuing their dreams.

GLOSSARY

absence seizure—A type of seizure in which a person stares for a few seconds, does not lose consciousness, and returns to the activity going on before the seizure.

acupuncture—A form of alternative medicine in which very small needles are inserted into specific areas of the body to relieve pain or treat illnesses.

anti-epileptic drugs—Medication used to prevent or treat seizures. These are sometimes called anti-convulsant or anti-seizure medications.

atonic seizure—A quick and sudden seizure in which a person's muscles give way.

aura—A warning felt by some people just before a seizure starts.

axon—The long extended part of a neuron that carries messages toward other neurons.

Central Nervous System (CNS)—The brain and spinal cord.

consciousness—Being awake and aware of one's surroundings.

dendrites—The branching structure of a neuron that receives messages.

diagnose—To identify an illness based on results of tests.

diazepam—A type of medication used to relax muscles or to relieve anxiety.

electroencephalograph (EEG)—A machine used for tracing and recording the electrical activity of the brain by means of electrodes attached to the scalp.

epilepsy—A chronic neurological disorder that is characterized by seizures.

frontal lobe—The top, front regions of each of the cerebral hemispheres of the brain. They are used for reasoning, emotions, judgment, and voluntary movement.

focal seizure—A seizure that involves only one region of the brain.

generalized seizure—A seizure that involves the entire brain, causing a person to lose consciousness.

glial cells—Nerve cells that form a supporting network for the neurons in the brain.

***grand mal* seizure**—An older term for a generalized, tonic clonic seizure.

hypothalamus—A region in the upper part of the brain stem that acts as a relay to control body temperature, sleep, moods, hormonal body processes, hunger, and thirst.

ketogenic diet—A high-fat diet that produces ketones in the blood. Ketones act to calm seizures and many young children can control difficult seizures with this diet.

myoclonic seizure—A type of seizure in which the person may jerk and twitch but will not lose consciousness.

neurology—The study of the nervous system and its disorders.

neuron—A nerve cell.

neurotransmitters—Chemicals in the brain that aid in transmitting signals and messages back and forth between neurons.

partial seizure—The most common type of seizure. A person undergoing a partial seizure will not lose consciousness or have distorted muscle movements but will see, hear, or smell things that are not really there.

Petit mal **seizure**—An older term for an absence seizure.

pons—The part of the brain stem that joins the hemispheres of the cerebellum and connects the cerebrum with the cerebellum.

seizure—A sudden, abnormal electrical discharge in the brain.

side effect—An unwanted result of using a particular medication.

soma—The cell body of the neuron that contains the nucleus.

synapse—A small gap between one neuron and another that allows a signal to cross.

temporal lobe—The region at the lower side of each cerebral hemisphere that contains the brain's centers for hearing and memory.

thalamus—A small structure at the top of the brain stem that serves as a relay center for sensory information, pain, attention, and alertness.

tonic-clonic seizure—A type of seizure in which the person may lose consciousness, fall down, and experience jerking and twitching of the muscles. These seizures last for two to three minutes.

Vagus Nerve Stimulation (VNS)—A surgical device implanted under the skin that helps control seizures.

FIND OUT MORE

Organizations

American Epilepsy Society

342 North Main Street

West Hartford, CT 06117

860-586-7505

www.aesnet.org

This is a Web site that helps health-care workers communicate with each other about epilepsy. It has good information on medication and side effects, new research, and help finding a neurology specialist by zip code.

Epilepsy Foundation of America

4351 Garden City Drive Suite 406

Landover, MD 20785

1-800-EFA-1000

www.efa.org

This organization is dedicated to helping people with epilepsy find answers, learn about new research, therapies, surgery, and medications. Visit the Answer place pages to find out about history, seizure and epilepsy types, a glossary, and epilepsy facts.

National Institutes of Health National Institute of Neurological Disorders and Stroke (NINDS)

Building 31, Room 8A06

Bethesda, MD 20892

301- 496-5924

www.ninds.nih.gov

This is the Web site of the United States government agency that studies brain and nervous system disorders and provides education to the public. You can order pamphlets and read about new developments in epilepsy research.

Books

Dudley, Mark Edward. *Epilepsy*. Berkely Heights, NJ: Enslow Publishers, 2001.

Goodfellow, Gregory. *Epilepsy*. San Diego, CA: Lucent Books, 2001.

Haugen, Hayley Mitchell. *Epilepsy*. Detroit, MI: Thomson/Gale 2005.

Routh, Kristina, *Epilepsy*. Chicago, Il: Heinemann Library, 2004.

Web Sites

Epilepsy Action–British Epilepsy Organization
http://www.epilepsy.org.uk

Epilepsy Canada
http://www.epilepsy.ca

Epilepsy.Com—Kid Zone
http://www.epilepsy.com/kids/kids.html

Epilepsy Foundation of Southern California
http://www.epilepsy-socalif.org/

Epilepsy Institute
http://www.epilepsyinstitute.org

National Information Center for Children and Youth with
    Disabilities
http://www.nichcy.org

Neuroscience for Kids
http://faculty.washington.edu/chudler/neurok.html

INDEX

ABOUT THE AUTHOR

Ruth Bjorklund lives on Bainbridge Island, across Puget Sound from Seattle, Washington, with her husband, two children, two big hound dogs, and a cat. Her daughter has a seizure disorder, and everyone in the family appreciates the care and support they have received from their community.